KLUTZ
APRIL 1 02
PALO ALTO

Handmade Cards

Simple Designs for Beautiful Cards

Anne Akers Johnson

KLUTZ is a kids' company staffed entirely by real human beings. We began our corporate life in 1977 in an office we shared with a Chevrolet Impala. Today we've outgrown our founding garage, but Palo Alto, California, remains Klutz galactic headquarters. For those of you who collect corporate mission statements, here's ours:

Create wonderful things. Be good. Have fun.

Write Us We would love to hear your comments regarding this or any of our books. We have many!

KLUTZ® 455 Portage Avenue, Palo Alto, CA 94306   KLUTZ.com **Come on in!** OPEN 24 HOURS

Additional Copies and More Supplies

For the location of your nearest Klutz retailer, call (650) 857-0888. Should they be tragically out of stock, additional copies of this book and the entire library of 100% Klutz certified books are available in our mail order catalog. See back page.

Table of contents

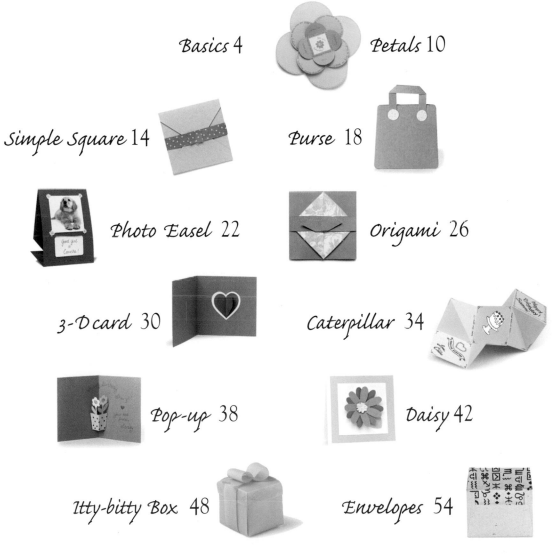

Most of the tools you need to make your own cards are included with this book.

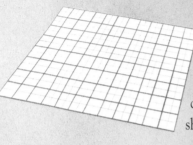

Measuring grid:
Better than a ruler.
Really. Use this to
measure your cards and to
draw straight lines. We'll
show you how on page 7.

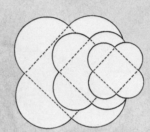

Templates:
Trace around the templates
to mark your paper before
cutting. The templates
also show you where to
score fold lines.

Folding tool: Use the folding
tool to score your cards before folding,
and to crease them after. It's a small
thing that makes a big difference.

Paper: There
are two weights of paper.
The thick stuff is called cardstock;
the lighter stuff is text paper. We'll always
tell you which is best for you project.

Portfolio: Store all your papers
and templates in this box to
protect them.

Getting

Glue: Either stick or liquid glue will work for most projects. For some things, like the daisy, liquid glue holds better. We'll be sure to tell you if this matters.

WHITE GLUE

glue stick

Scissors

Pencil

Craft knife: This is only necessary for a few cards, so don't worry if you don't have one yet. You can buy these in stationery, craft and art stores.

Started

More paper

Once you start making your own cards, you won't want to stop. You can find a good variety of paper at art and craft stores. Sometimes it's already cut into pieces like ours; other times it's available in big sheets that you have to cut down yourself.

But don't limit yourself to store-bought paper. If you look around, you'll find lots of great paper waiting to be reused. Make an envelope out of the Sunday funnies, save shopping bags with cool patterns printed on them, cut pictures out of old cards, wrapping paper or magazines to decorate your cards. Once you start looking, you'll find good paper everywhere.

Basic Cardmaking

We've provided templates for two envelopes, a rectangle and a square. If you plan on mailing your cards, you'll need to be sure your cards fit into one of these. It's a good rule to make your cards at least $\frac{1}{4}$ inch smaller than its envelope.

These cards will fit in your envelopes:

Square card

Finished size:
$4\frac{1}{2}$ x $4\frac{1}{2}$ inches

Cut your paper to
9 x $4\frac{1}{2}$ inches
and fold in half.

Note: It costs extra to mail a square envelope. Check with the post office before you drop one in the mail. You'll find more details about envelopes on pages 54–57.

Rectangular card

Finished size:
$4\frac{1}{2}$ x 6 inches

Cut your paper to 9 x 6 inches and fold in half.

Measuring

Your measuring grid makes it really easy to measure because you can mark two dimensions at the same time. Pull it out now and practice measuring out a card. For this example we'll measure the paper needed to make a 4½-inch square card.

1 Find a big-enough piece of paper and lay your grid over it. Measure 9 inches from the end and 4½ inches from the side.

Hold the grid in place, then use a pencil to trace lightly around the edges of the grid.

2 Cut your card out, then erase the pencil lines if they still show.

4½"

9"

Folding

Always use your folding tool when you're folding cardstock. It just looks better.

1 To fold the card you just measured, place your grid over the paper so it measures 4 ½ inches.

Hold the grid firmly in place and use the metal loop on your folding tool to score a fold line in the paper.

2 Remove the grid and fold the card along the scored line.

3 Finally, lay your folding tool flat on top of the card and run it along the fold to make a nice neat crease.

Folder is flat.

4½"

Be sure the paper edge lines up perfectly with the 4 ½-inch line on the grid.

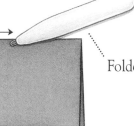

Using a Template

The templates that come with this book make it really easy to make beautiful cards.

1 Lay the template over a big-enough piece of paper. Hold it in place and draw lightly around the edges with a pencil.

(The Pop-up template is a little different.)

Place your template close to the edge of the paper so you're left with good-sized scraps.

2 The dashed lines on the template show you the fold lines. Take the template off the paper, and use your measuring grid to score straight lines that match the dashed lines on the template.

Petals

This card unfolds into a
pretty flower, then closes
up to make its own envelope.

You will need:

- 3 pieces of cardstock
  (It's nice if they're
  different colors.)
- Glue
- All 3 petal templates

Decorate your card
with a rubber stamp.

You're invited to a movie night. Fran's going to bring her awsome. Rhonda's coming. chocolate chip cookies. Bring or B square! Bring your favorite movie. We'll eat pizza and popcorn. My house! When else? bringing the same movie she always brings.

My house!
Saturday
7:00
When else?
See you Saturday!

1 Use your templates to outline one petal of each size: small, medium and large. Cut them out, erase any pencil lines that show, then score all the fold lines with your folding tool.

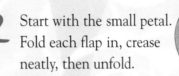

2 Start with the small petal. Fold each flap in, crease neatly, then unfold.

3 Close the card by folding each flap in, moving in a circle around the card as shown.

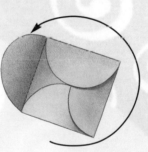

4 Lift the first flap and tuck the edge of the last flap under it.

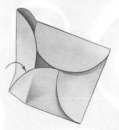

5 Next, glue the small card onto the medium card so it looks just like the picture.

Close the medium-sized card in the same way you did the small one.

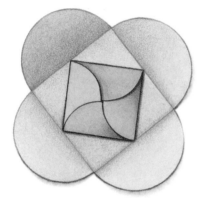

Variation: Glue two flaps down to turn a single petal into a heart-shaped envelope...

To:
Laura

...then seal it with a sticker.

6 Next, glue the medium card onto the large petal card in the same way.

Close the large petal, then leave the card under a heavy book to dry for a few minutes.

You can also make single petal cards. Only the large one is big enough to go through the mail.

Cutting nice curves

Point your scissors away from you and turn the paper as you cut. Don't turn the scissors.

It's easiest to cut *into* tight angles...

...then continue cutting in the direction that's most comfortable for you.

Simple Square

This card folds up to make its own envelope. Very simple. Very classy.

You will need:

- 1 piece of cardstock
- 1 piece of text paper
- Simple Square template (same as the square envelope)

1 Use your template to outline the pattern on a big-enough piece of paper. Cut it out.

2 Score the four fold lines.

3 Fold the side flaps in and crease well...

4 ...then fold the top and bottom in.

Make a paper band to hold it closed (page 16).

Happy Birthday Camille!

♥

Margaret

Good for 1

birthday sundae!

Glue slightly smaller squares of contrasting paper into your card to make a frame.

To make a paper band

1 Cut a piece of paper 1 inch wide and 12 inches long.

2 Wrap the band around your card so that the ends overlap at its center.

3 Arrange the ends so the bottom layer peeks out below the top layer. Draw a line on the top layer 1 inch in from the end. Start at the top of the band and go to the middle. Make a mark on the bottom layer in line with this mark. Look at the picture to be sure you've got it right.

4 Lift the top layer out of the way, and draw a line on the bottom layer running from the little mark you just made up to the center of the band.

5 Make a cut along each line…

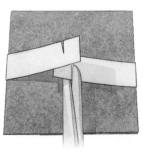

You can also tie your square closed with a pretty ribbon...

...or seal it with a sticker and it's ready to mail.

6 ...then connect the two ends of the band by sliding the cuts together as shown.

purse

You will need:

- 1 piece of cardstock for the purse
- 1 piece of cardstock or text paper for the card
- Glue
- Purse template (one piece)

Write a message on a simple card and tuck it into this little purse.

The purse fits in the rectangular envelope.

1 The easiest way to make the purse front is to draw around the four shaded corners of the template, then connect the lines using your measuring grid.

The front will look like this:

...and the back like this.

2 Set the front aside for now and work on the back. Use your measuring grid to score all the flaps on the purse back.

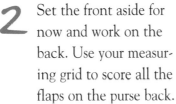

Use scalloped scissors to make a pretty edge on your purse.

Make a purse without a flap. This one has two handles.

This purse was cut out of an old paper bag.

Cut a flap out of contrasting paper and glue it over the original.

Glue a button on the flap.

3 Fold the side and bottom flaps into the center of the purse. Crease well.

4 Now fold the top flap down, crease, then unfold. Easy.

5 Run a little glue along the side and bottom flaps...

6 ...then lay the purse front over the back and press down.

Wipe off any glue that seeps out the edges.

7 Fold the top flap back down, then carefully place the purse under a heavy book to dry while you make the handle (instructions on page 21).

8 After you've added the handle, cut and fold a card with a finished size of 3 ½ inches square. Tuck the card into the purse.

Karen

Variation: Punch holes in the purse so you can tie it closed with a ribbon.

To make the handle:

1 Cut a strip of paper ½ inch wide and 6 inches long.

2 Measure in 2 ¼ inches from each end and make a small dot with your pencil.

3 Now fold both ends at the dots so they point straight down.

4 Put a little glue on each end of the handle, then glue it to the back of the purse.

Photo easel

This card opens into an easel—perfect for sending a favorite photo.

You will need:

- 1 piece of cardstock
- Glue
- Craft knife
- A photo cut no larger than 4 x 5½. Smaller is OK.

Always be careful when cutting with a craft knife.

Decorate the front of the card with a sticker...

a scrap of wrapping paper...

or a rubber stamp.

1 Measure and cut one piece of cardstock 4¼ x 12 inches long and another piece 4¼ x 4¼ inches long.

12"

4¼"

4¼"

4¼"

2 Set the small piece aside for now and work on the long piece. Score the card 6 inches from the end, then measure and cut a point to match the picture.

6"

2"

score

cut

cut

2"

2"

3 Fold the card in half, crease well, then fold it back the other way. It should fold easily in both directions.

4 Go back to the small piece of paper. Draw a line that runs 1 inch from the bottom edge, and 1 inch from each side. Check the picture to be sure you've got it right, then carefully cut along the line with your craft knife.

1"

1" 1"

5 Now score a fold line 1 inch from the top.

score

1"

6 Fold the paper along this line, unfold, then fold back the other way.

7 Glue this 1-inch flap to the flat end of the card. Make sure the short flap still folds easily in both directions.

8 Fold the card so the short flap is on the inside and the pointed flap on the outside. Place under a heavy book for a few minutes while the glue sets.

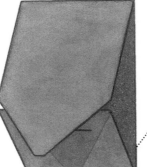

The glued-together seam is on the back.

9 When the glue is dry, open the card and attach a photo to the inside. Double-stick tape works well for this.

glue picture here

10 To turn the card into an easel, open both flaps to the back and tuck the pointed end into the cut on the short flap.

Origami

This card is inspired by a Japanese paper fold. It fits in either the square or rectangular envelope.

You will need:

- 1 piece of cardstock
- 1 piece of text paper
- Glue
- Origami template (1 piece)

This card is very easy to make. Just be sure to measure carefully.

1 Use the template to cut two pieces of text paper. Cut another piece of text paper 1 x 11 inches long for the paper band. Set these aside for now.

2 Cut a piece of cardstock 4½ x 9 inches. Be precise. It makes all the difference.

4½"

9"

3 Score a fold line 2¼ inches from each end.

score

score

2¼"

2¼"

4 Fold the ends into the center and press flat.

These edges just meet.

Liz -
I know tomorrow is a big day for you. Just wanted to say Good Luck! You're going to do great!
♥ Jill

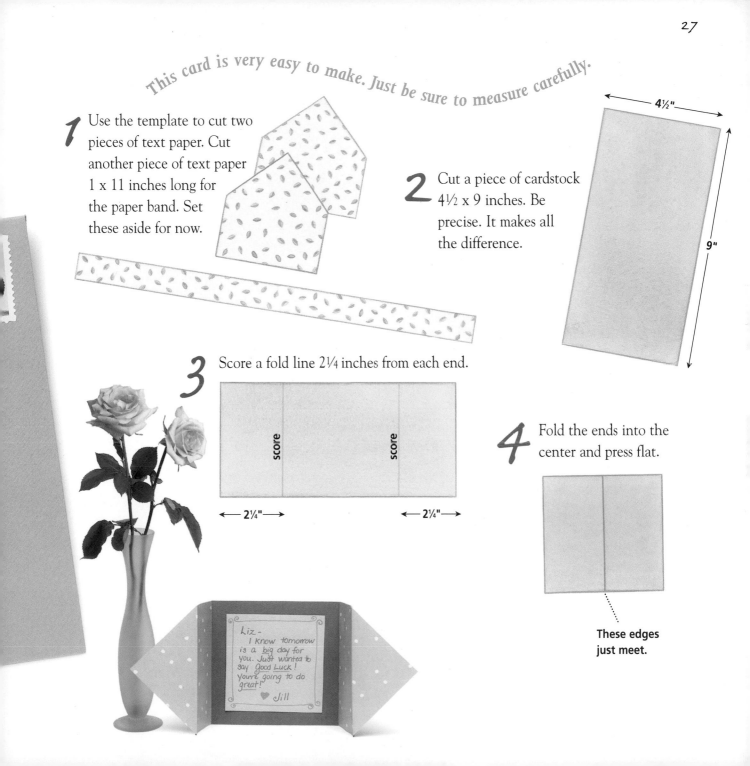

5 Cut a super-thin strip off each flap, just enough to make a little gap between them, about this wide:

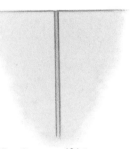

Don't worry if it's not perfectly straight. It won't show.

6 Run a line of glue around the inside of one of the flaps...

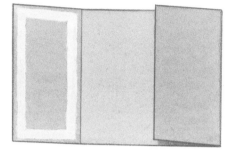

7 ...then glue one of the pieces of text paper onto it so its edge just touches the fold line.

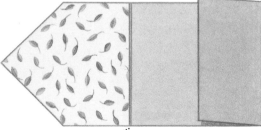

Fold line

8 Fold the flap back into the center...

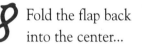

9 ...then fold the text paper back along the edge of the card. Press flat.

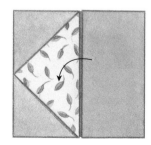

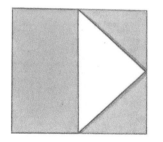

10 Glue the remaining piece of text paper to the other flap in the same way.

11 Follow the directions on page 16 to make a paper band to go around the card.

3-D Card

This simple card opens to a pretty, 3-D design. Choose either the butterfly or the heart template for your design. We used the heart in the instructions.

You will need:

- An already-made card, square or rectangular
- A scrap of cardstock for the heart or butterfly
- Glue
- A craft knife
- One of the 3-D templates, the heart or the butterfly

Suki- last weekend was so fun! i can't wait

teach again- you're the best!

thanks!
love, corie

to go back to the

1 Trace two hearts onto your cardstock and cut them out. Set the hearts aside for now.

2 Draw a 2¼-inch line down the center of the card starting at least an inch from the top (if your card is 4½ inches wide, the center is 2¼ inches from the side).

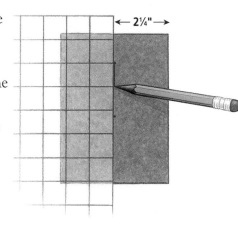

← 2¼" →

3 Open the card up and use your craft knife to cut along the line.

4 Now go back to the hearts. Score each one down the middle.

Fold in half. Crease well, then unfold.

Always be extremely careful when cutting with a craft knife. Put an old magazine or some newspapers under the card while you cut.

5 To assemble your card, poke one heart through the cut in the front...

6 ...then fold it in half so one side is inside the card and the other is outside.

7 Now poke the second heart through the cut and fold it in half to make the other side of the heart.

8 Make sure the heart is arranged so it will slip easily through the cut once it's glued in place.

The cut should be longer than both the highest and lowest point on your heart.

9 Now open the card up so you can see the inside hearts. Spread glue over them both...

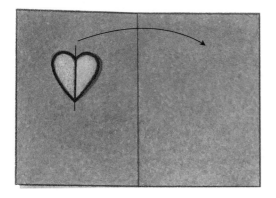

10 ...then close the card and press it flat while the glue dries.

11 Once the glue is dry, open the card to see your 3-D heart. Tuck the heart back through the cut to close it.

CaTeRPiLLaR

The caterpillar looks like an ordinary card when it's closed. Once open, you'll see it's anything but ordinary.

SUMMER BREAK

You will need:

- 2 sheets of text paper
- Glue

Decorate your card with photos or scraps of paper.

Kristen, Pauli, Traci, KYM

We had a blast! The big trip to san Diego was tons of fun. (we blew all our $$ on jewelry & ice cream). And don't forget the sand volleyball (RED TEAM RULES). See you guys next summer! xxoo

THIS GIRL HATES HAVING HER PIC. TAKEN.

you go, Cowgirl

BEN, LISHA, TRACI, REBECCA HANGING OUT ON JULY 4th

SUMMER TOP-TEN:
1. orange sherbet 2. the beach 3. kristen's new convertible 4. cherry lipgloss 5. san diego! 6. midnight movies 7. volleyball 8. flip-flops 9. no school 10. sun-glasses

Lisa

(yeah, right.) I'd rather be in math class.

Rebecca & Danielle

Marie & Adam

MATTHEW the CAT

Could I be any cuter?

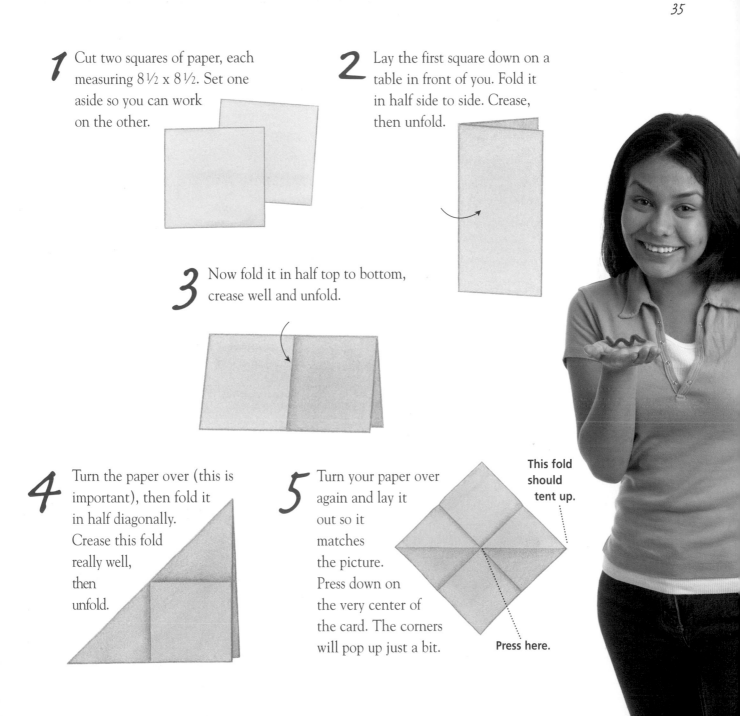

1 Cut two squares of paper, each measuring 8½ x 8½. Set one aside so you can work on the other.

2 Lay the first square down on a table in front of you. Fold it in half side to side. Crease, then unfold.

3 Now fold it in half top to bottom, crease well and unfold.

4 Turn the paper over (this is important), then fold it in half diagonally. Crease this fold really well, then unfold.

5 Turn your paper over again and lay it out so it matches the picture. Press down on the very center of the card. The corners will pop up just a bit.

This fold should tent up.

Press here.

6 Bring the top corner down to meet the bottom corner. Push the two side corners in so they meet in the center.

7 When this is done right, you'll have a nice little square. Run your folding tool over the whole thing to press the folds really flat.

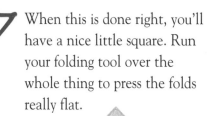

8 Fold the second square of paper in exactly the same way.

9 Open the first square up and outline the bottom panel with glue...

10 ...then open the second square, turn it over and lay its top panel over the gluey panel of the first.

11 Press the two panels together.

12 Fold the caterpillar flat and leave it under a heavy book for a few minutes. When it's dry, write on it or decorate it any way you want.

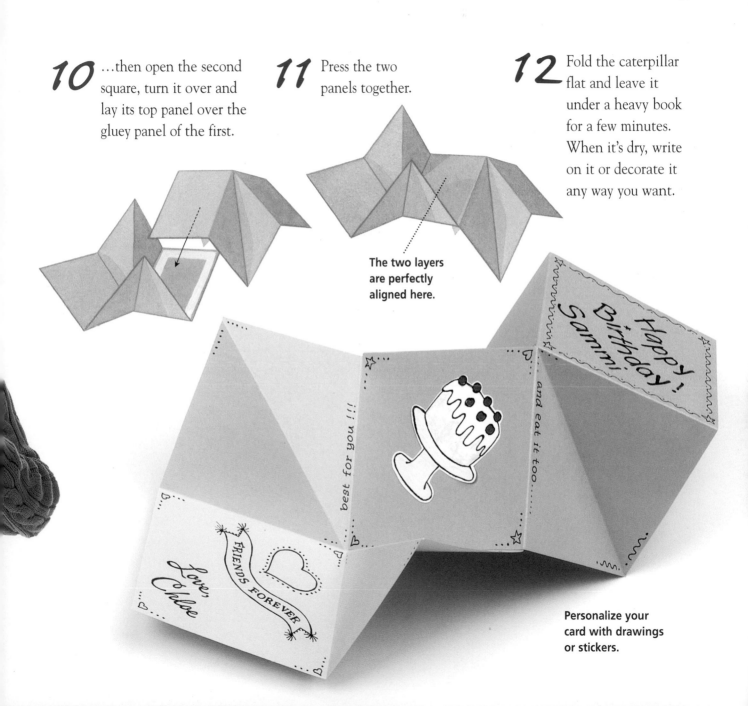

The two layers are perfectly aligned here.

Happy Birthday! Sammi

and eat it too

best for you !!!

FRIENDS FOREVER

Love, Chloe

Personalize your card with drawings or stickers.

Pop-up

It's easier than you think to make your own pop-up card.

You will need:

- An already-folded card, square or rectangular
- Three scraps of cardstock: one color for the stem, one for the flower and one for the flower pot.
- Glue
- Pop-up templates (1 piece)

Happy Birthday Ines!

Hope this is your best year yet!

love,
Nancy

The pop-up template is different from all the others.
Read the directions printed on this template before you use it.

1 Cut out 2 flowers, 1 flower pot and 1 of each stem.

2 Glue the flowers onto the tops of the stems. Easy.

The stems go about half-way up the back of flowers.

3 Score fold lines onto the flower pot to match those on the template. Fold the two flaps back.

4 Fold the flowerpot in half, crease well, then unfold. The side that tents up is the front.

5 Next, unfold the pot and glue a flower onto each half. Glue them to the back of the pot. It's OK if they overlap a little in the middle.

The single leaf goes on this side.

Make sure the flowers don't stick out past the outside fold lines.

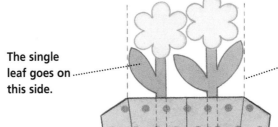

6 Now fold the flower pot tabs back along the fold line.

Use colored pens to draw details onto the flowers.

7 Put a little glue on the tabs, then glue the pot flat onto the card so the fold line on the flowerpot lines up with the fold line on the card.

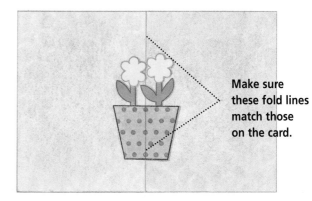

Make sure these fold lines match those on the card.

8 Hold the flower-
pot in place while
the glue dries,
then close the
card and press the
whole thing flat.

9 When you open
the card, the flow-
ers will pop out.

daisy

You will need:

- 1 already-folded card (square or rectangular)

- Scraps of text paper for the daisy: green for the leaves, and 2–3 colors for the flower

- Daisy template

- Glue (liquid is best)

This card doesn't mail well, but it's great to give to someone personally.

This card is easier than it looks, especially after you've made your first one. The daisy is made up of two petal rings. Vary your flowers by changing the color and size of the petal rings you use. For your first daisy, use one small and one large petal ring. It'll be easier to follow the directions.

1 Trace and cut out a large and small ring of petals, a leaf and three base leaves. Cut, score and fold a card. Either square or rectangle is fine.

2 For the center, use your grid to measure out a strip of text paper $1/2$ inch wide, and 6 inches long.

3 Cut a fringe along the length of the center strip as shown.

4 Start at one end and roll the strip around itself tightly. Don't worry if it's not perfectly round at first, just press it into shape and keep rolling. It'll turn out fine.

Leave the bottom third of the strip uncut so it stays in one piece.

5 Glue the end down and hold it in place until the glue sets.

6 Press down on the fringe to spread it out as shown. Don't be timid: Smoosh it so it matches the picture.

7 Next, assemble the petals. Place a dot of glue on the little tab that falls between the two widely spaced petals (better look at the picture here)…

Use scalloped scissors to cut a fancy-edged square to frame the daisy.

…then pull the tab under the next petal to close the gap in the petal ring. Pinch this tab firmly until the glue sets. You'll notice that the petals are gently cupping now.

9 Glue the second ring of petals in the same way.

10 When the glue has dried, stack the petal rings, then push the center roll down through their centers.

11 Carefully turn the flower upside down, and glue the three leaf bases to the underside of a petal and down the stem. Don't worry when they aren't symmetrical. They just won't be.

Leave about 1/2 inch of the leaf hanging off the bottom.

Attach a daisy card to a package and skip the bow.

12

Now fold the leaf bases out flat, and put a little glue on each. Put some glue on the center coil for good measure.

13

Gently press the daisy down onto the card, making sure the three leaf bases are flat against the card. Leave the card to dry for a few minutes.

14 Find your leaf, fold it in half to crease it, then unfold it. The edges will cup up gently.

15 Run a little glue along the underside of the leaf...

16 ...then gently tuck it under the flower on the card. You may need to hold it for a moment while the glue dries. Beautiful!

We added a square of yellow and a slightly smaller square of blue to frame this daisy.

itty-bitty box

...opens into a card.

You will need:

- 2 pieces of cardstock
  (for the box and lid)
- 1 piece of text paper
  (for the bow)
- A little glue (Liquid works
  best for this one.)

Write a
message inside
your box.

1 Trace the box onto the cardstock, then cut it out and score all the fold lines. Be sure to score through the dots you marked on the paper.

2 Using your folding tool, crease each fold line well, then unfold.

3 Now place the box on a table in front of you with the outside facing down. Stand the top and left sides up, gently pushing the in-between triangular piece in as you do.

To make the box:

4 Hold the two sides together with one hand, and crease the triangle right down to the bottom corner.

5 Repeat this all the way around the box. Set the box aside for now and work on the lid.

You can tie your box with a real ribbon...

Making the lid

...or make a simple paper band (page 16).

This bow is made of translucent paper.

1 Trace the lid pattern onto your paper, cut it out and carefully score all the fold lines.

2 Lay the lid down in front of you with the outside face down. Fold each flap at the scored lines, crease them with your folder, then unfold.

3 Stand the top and left flaps up so they just touch, pushing the little triangular piece toward the center. Pinch the little triangle to flatten it.

4 Crease all four corners this way.

5 Next spread a little glue along the top flap…

**Put some glue on
these triangles too.**

6 …then lift the top and side flaps, making sure to push the little triangles in.

7 Fold the gluey flap down, being sure to cover the triangular pieces. Pinch the flap until the glue sets or use a paper clip to hold it in place.

8 Now put some glue on the bottom flap…

9 …and assemble this side in the same way.

10 Put some glue on the two remaining flaps and fold them down into place.

11 To assemble your box, fold all the flaps up…

12 …then put the lid on to hold it closed.

Put a surprise inside the box.

Celebrate!

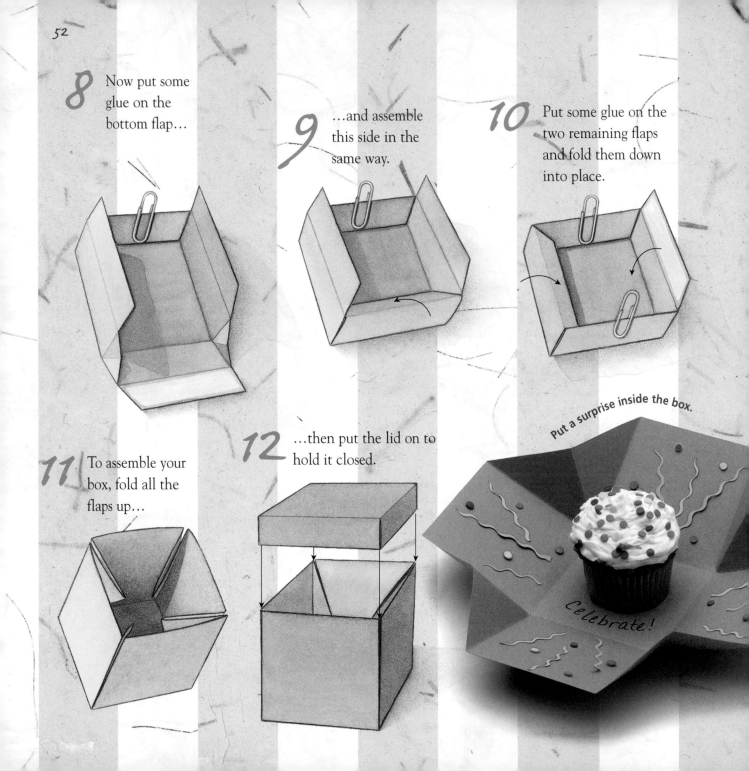

To make the bow:

1 Cut two bows out of text paper. Gently bend the end of each back, so that its notches align.

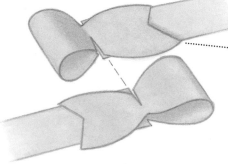

Make sure the short ends are on top and the two notched sides face each other.

2 Carefully slide the two pieces together.

You might have to cut the notch a little deeper to make the edges of the two pieces match up right.

3 Pinch the center of the bow against the top of the box to hold it in place.

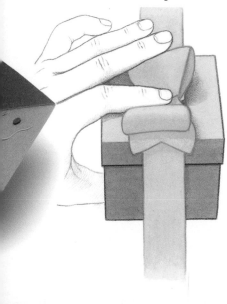

4 Turn the box over and wrap one end of the ribbon around to the bottom as shown. Put a little glue on this end.

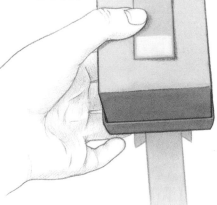

5 Now wrap the other end around so it overlaps the gluey piece. Hold in place until the glue is dry.

Envelopes

It's easy to make envelopes to match your cards. Choose either the square or the rectangular template. Remember that it costs a little extra to mail a square envelope.

You will need:

- 1 piece of text paper for each envelope
- Glue
- One of the envelope templates (The square envelope uses the same template as the Simple Square.)

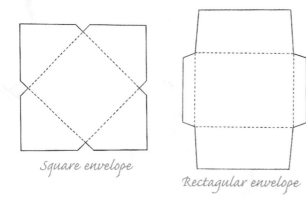

Square envelope   Rectagular envelope

The two envelopes are assembled in pretty much the same way.

Square:
Fits a card 4 ¾ inches square or smaller.

1

Use the template to mark your paper, then cut the envelope out and score all the fold lines.

Rectangle:
Fits a card measuring 4 ½ x 6 ¼ or smaller.

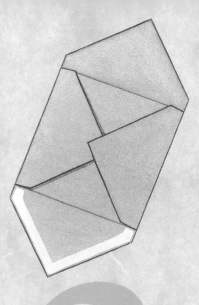

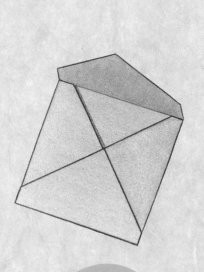

If you use printed paper for your envelope, you might need to glue a plain piece of paper onto the front for the address.

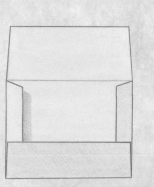

To:
Emma Anderson
455 Portage Ave.
Palo Alto, CA 94306

2

Fold the two side flaps in to the center, then run a little glue along the edges of the bottom flap.

3

Fold the bottom flap into place. Finish by folding the top flap down and creasing it neatly.

4

Seal the envelope with glue or make your own envelope glue (page 57).

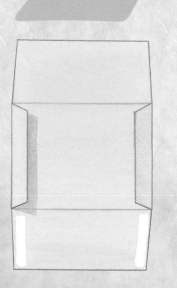

To make an envelope look lined, use printed paper with pattern folded to the inside.

Variations:

If you want to mail a square card, but don't want to pay extra postage, make this special envelope. Your card needs to be 4½ inches square or smaller.

1 Cut and score a rectangular envelope. Lay the envelope in front of you so the short flaps are on the top and bottom.

2 Place your card on the unfolded envelope, so that its top edge is just below the top fold line. Draw a light pencil line under the bottom of the card.

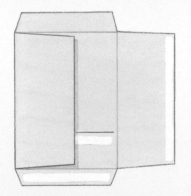

3 Set the card aside and run a skinny line of glue across the envelope about ¼ inch below the pencil line.

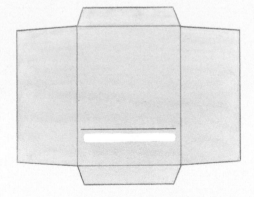

4 Fold the left flap in. Run a little glue along the edge of the right and bottom flaps. Fold the right flap in.

5 Then fold the bottom flap up. Press down on all the glued-together places so they stick.

Don't forget to press down here.

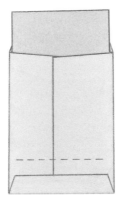

6 When your envelope is dry, you can slip a card into it. The glued-together part will keep the card from sliding to the bottom.

To make this envelope for a rectangular card, assemble it in the same way, but skip the line of glue on the inside.

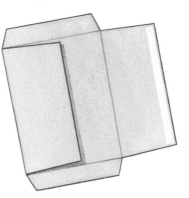

Envelope Glue

This recipe makes a clear glue for your envelopes. After it dries you can remoisten it, and seal your envelope.

- 2 Tablespoons white glue
- 1 Tablespoon white vinegar
- a small paint brush (In a pinch, your finger will work fine.)

Mix the glue and vinegar together in a small bowl or paper cup until well blended.

Use a small paint brush (or your finger) to smear a line of glue along the edge of your envelope flap.

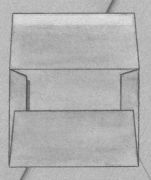

Let the glue dry completely, then store the envelope in a dry place until you're ready to seal it.

Credits

Book Design:
Jamison Design,
  Nevada City, CA

Art Direction:
Jill Turney

Photography:
Richard Reader
Peter Fox
Katrine Naleid

Illustration:
Vally Hennings
Darwin Hennings

Caterpillar Snapshots:
Thomas Heinser
Marcy Malloy

Calligraphy:
Barbara Callow,
  represented by
  Linda de Moreto
Monica Dengo
Liz Hutnick

Template Design:
Maria Seamans
Keeli McCarthy
Kate Paddock

Sticker Art:
Theresa Hutnick

Editorial Assistance:
Corie Thompson

Models:
Ernestine Balisi
Christina Belen
Hillary Benson
Larken Bonham
Sarah Burke
Cara Chronis
Christina Foung
Lauren Hobstetter
Kristyn Loy
Angelica Montes
Jessica Ortiz
Kristin Rapinchuk
Elizabeth Rose

Alicia Sheppard
Kendra Sutherland
Katherine Svetlichny
Danya Tamor
Kyleen Wolfson
Genevieve Yang
Erin Zee
Concha y Toro
  Montgomery
  (Good dog!)

Thanks to all the card
makers at Klutz for
their generous help.

More Great Books From Klutz

A Book of Artrageous Projects

Bead Rings

Squashing Flowers, Squeezing Leaves: A Nature Press & Book

Hair: A Book of Braiding & Styles

Making Mini-Books

Tissue Paper Flowers

The Body Book: Recipes for Natural Body Care

• CUT OUT • FILL IN • ADD STAMP • MAIL • WAIT IMPATIENTLY •

Klutz Catalog!

You can order the entire library of 100% Klutz certified books and a diverse collection of other things we happen to like from The Klutz Catalog. It is, in all modesty, unlike any other catalog — and it's yours for the asking.

Who are you?

Name: _____ Age: _____ ❑ Too high to count ○ Boy ○ Girl

Address: _____

City: _____ State: _____ Zip: _____

My Bright Ideas!

Tell us what you think of this book: _____

_____

What would you like us to write a book about? _____

_____

❑ Check this box if you want us to send you The Klutz Catalog.

If you're a grown-up who'd like to hear about new Klutz stuff, give us your e-mail address and we'll stay in touch.

E-mail address: _____

KLUTZ.com
Come on in! OPEN 24 HOURS

Handmade Cards

First Class
Postage
Here

KLUTZ®

455 Portage Avenue
Palo Alto, CA 94306